MEWBURN PARK
Homestead

A historic estate with a modern twist in the heart of Gippsland Victoria, offering you and your guests a perfect and relaxed wedding day. An unforgettable ceremony under a shady tree or at the historic Stables, breathtaking photo opportunities and a dreamy reception in our clear view marquee.

mewburnpark.com.au // info@mewburnpark.com.au

KINGS & THIEVES

POWERFUL WEDDING CHRONICLING
FOR THE RECKLESS AT HEART

CAPTURING ORGANIC MOMENTS FOR AMAZING COUPLES

michaelbriggs.com.au

Dwayne & Karl	**12**
Why Can't Men Hold Bouquets?	**20**
Jay & Jenna	**22**
Introducing, Shane Ave	**30**
Ian & Stephen	**34**
Things We Love	**42**
Lauren & Sam	**46**
Breaking Traditions	**53**
Matt & Zac - 10 Years of Marriage	**58**
Lily & Oscar	**64**
Katie & Kay	**68**
Rainbow Love	**76**
Abbey & Kate	**82**
Joel & Joseph	**90**
How to Choose Your Wedding Vendors	**99**
Dean & Sam	**100**
Lauren & Roya	**106**
Bobby & Joel	**110**
Brighton Romance	**114**
The Directory	**120**

Photography by Tanya Volt

We did it! Welcome to the launch edition of Dancing With Them Magazine.

If you don't already know our faces, we are Arlia (right) and Tara (left), two long term lovers who've been engaged for a smidge over three years. When Tara proposed to Arlia, we were quick to discover a wedding industry full of heteronormative, gendered, traditions, and expectations. We didn't see ourselves represented, and that was disheartening. We launched our other platform, Dancing With Her, to inspire other couples like us but always felt that we needed to extend what we were doing to include the wider LGBTQ+ community.

So, Dancing With Them was born. A publication that celebrates all LGBTQ+ love, authentically and with a whole lot of heart.

We wholeheartedly believe that all love deserves to be celebrated.

This Volume has so much love poured into it. The couples featured have shared some incredible stories of love, engagements, weddings, gender, and everything in between.

We get to explore one couple's journey through ten years of marriage and another as they transitioned gender during their relationship.

We get the opportunity to share some of the most beautiful weddings from around the world - from Dwayne and Karl's emotional Baltimore wedding ceremony to Ian and Stephan's dapper, two-tux, wedding in Canada.

Lauren & Roya's epic sunset proposal will have you tearing up with happiness and Dean and Sam's steamy at-home session, inspiring you to book your very own with your lover.

We are so proud of what this celebrates.

We know you're going to love it, cover to cover.

We want to take a quick opportunity to say a giant thankyou to the people that brought this issue to life. From the lovers who so openly shared their stories, photographers who have shared their art and the contributors and wedding professionals who helped these pages come to life in one way or another, thank you.

As always, thank you, reader. Thanks for supporting our work. Because of you, we can share these incredible stories of LGBTQ+ love with the world.

This volume is a community effort, and we are so, so, thankful.

Love,
Arlia & Tara
Founders of Dancing With Them

TUESDAY PHOTOGRAPHY

Based in Brisbane | Available Australia-wide

tuesdayphotography.com.au

EDITOR & CO-FOUNDER
Tara Baker

CREATIVE DIRECTOR & CO-FOUNDER
Arlia Hassell

WRITER
Sasha Sheehan

CONTRIBUTING PHOTOGRAPHERS
Love to the Core Photo, Eve Rox Photography, Bows and Lavender, Elvira Kalviste, Maryland Photography, Sara Hannagan Photography, Studio XIII Photography, Maria Bauer Photography, Marissa Solini Photography, Tuesday Photography, Widman Photography, Hannah Gilbert Photography, James Thorne, Be Here Be Now Photos and Films, Fox & Kin, Kristyn Taulane, Silk and Thorn, Stephanie Dreams Photography

FRONT COVER IMAGE
Love to the Core Photo
www.lovetothecorephoto.com

BACK COVER IMAGE
Eve Rox Photography
www.everoxphotography.com

SUBMISSIONS
www.dancingwiththem.com/submissions

ADVERTISING & WHOLESALE ENQUIRIES
partnerships@dancingwiththem.com

DANCING WITH THEM
P.O. Box 609
Coolangatta, QLD, 4225
Australia

JOIN OUR COMMUNITY
www.dancingwiththem.com
facebook.com/dancingwiththem
instagram.com/dancingwiththem
pinterest.com/dancingwiththem_mag

Dancing With Them acknowledges the Australian Aboriginal and Torres Strait Islander peoples of this nation. We acknowledge the people of the Bundjalung Nation whose Land on which our company is located and where we primarily conduct our business. We pay our respects to Ancestors and Elders, past, present and emerging. Dancing With Them is committed to honoring Australian Aboriginal and Torres Strait Islander Peoples unique cultural and spiritual relationships to the land, waters and seas and their rich contribution to society.

© 2020 Dancing With Them™

All rights reserved. Reproduction in whole or part without permission is strictly prohibited

ShaneAve.
SYDNEY

LEADERS IN MADE TO MEASURE SUITS AND SHIRTS FOR EVERYBODY

FREEDOM OF EXPRESSION

www.shaneave.com

Instagram | @shane.ave   Facebook | @aveshane1

BALTIMORE, UNITED STATES OF AMERICA

DWAYNE & KARL

PHOTOGRAPHY BY LOVE TO THE CORE PHOTO
www.lovetothecorephoto.com

dwayne
AND
karl
request your presence at their wedding
july nineteenth two thousand nineteen
at five fifteen in the evening
mt. washington mill dye house
1340 smith avenue
baltimore, md
dinner and dancing will follow

DWAYNE & KARL DISTILLERY
DA TEA
EST.
07.19.19

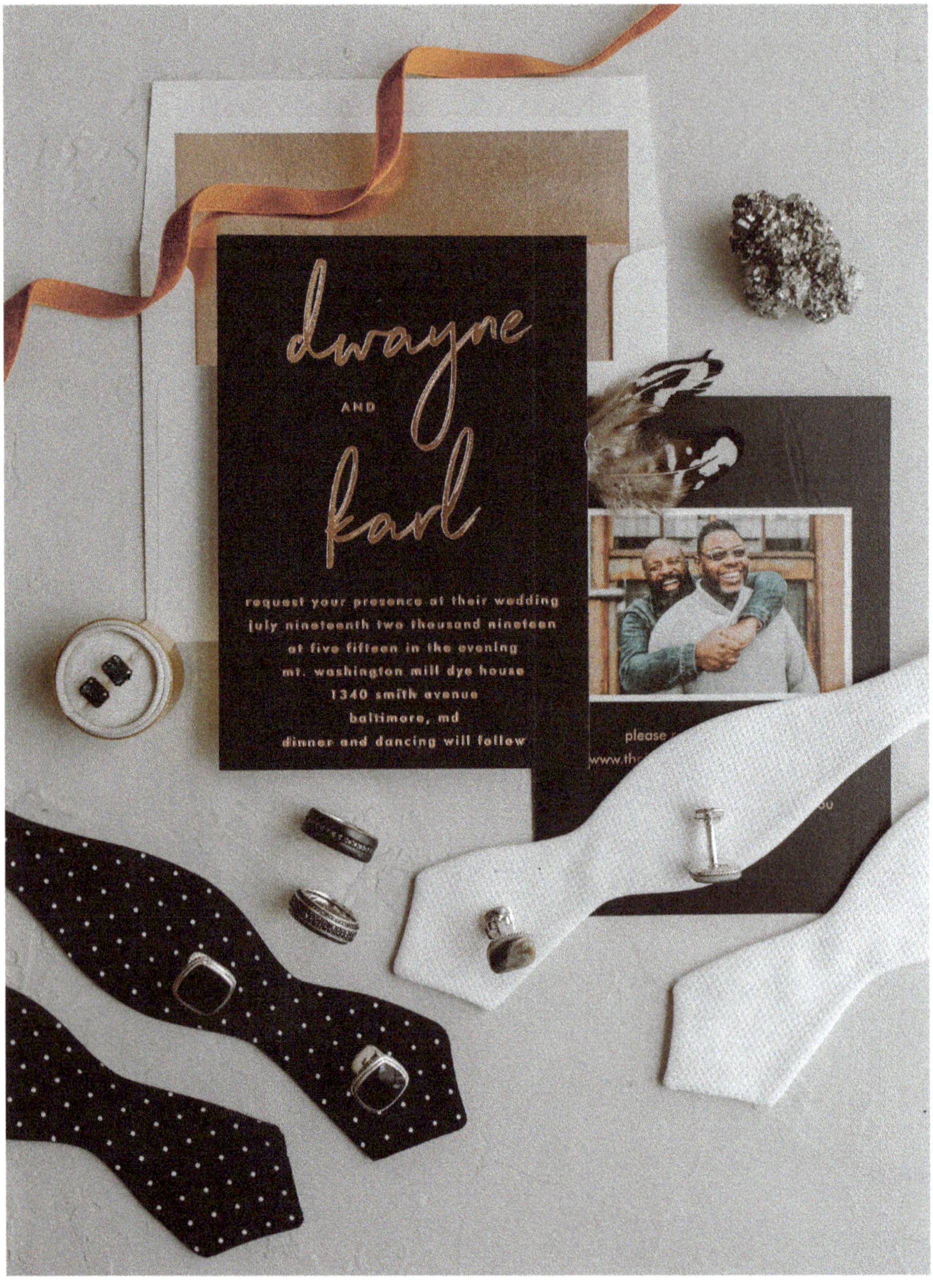

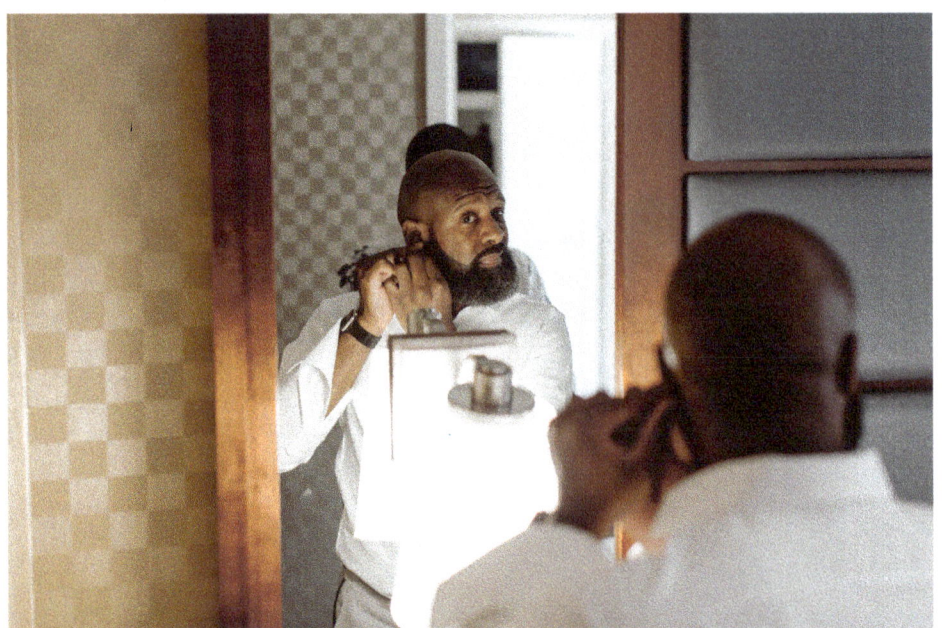

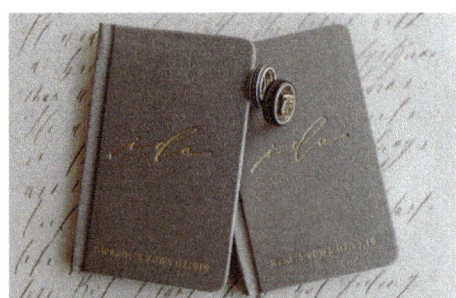

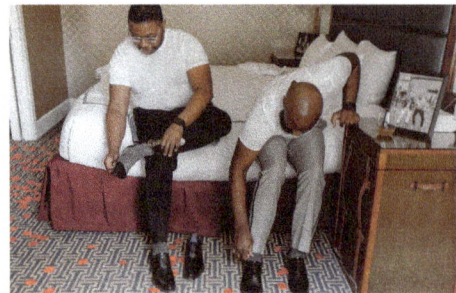

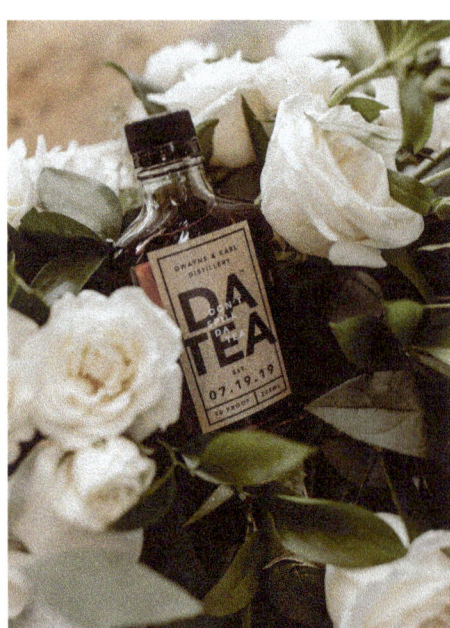

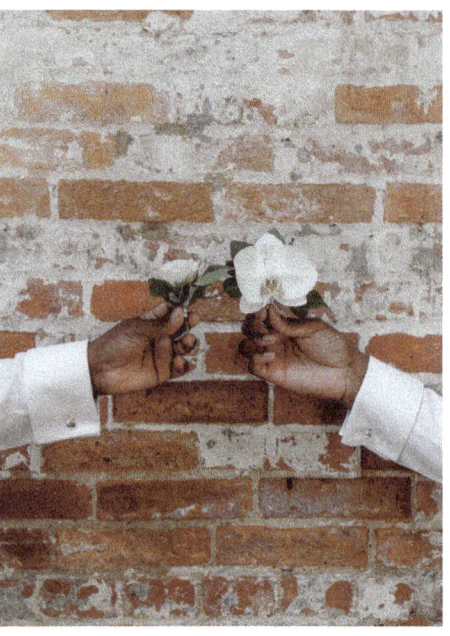

"Marriage is celebrating love for one another and the willingness to accept each other's strengths and weaknesses.

It's about sharing our individual outlooks and growing through our shared experiences.

Oddly enough, marriage means freedom to us. Freedom to live. Freedom to be our authentic selves and knowing that you have someone by your side who understands when no one else does.

Marriage is loving someone who loves, appreciates, and who gets you. It's loving someone who allows you to be you and has the desire to reciprocate for life.

Marriage is also having a built-in dinner and movie date for life - winning!"

It was only a short eight months after their engagement that Dwayne and Karl tied the knot in a heartfelt and perfect ceremony, surrounded by love.

Dwayne and Karl became a couple after sliding into one another's DMs over three years ago. Little did they know, that not long after, they would both start planning their proposals.

On the weekend after Thanksgiving, Dwayne decided to propose to Karl first. The couple spent the day visiting their favorite places to eat and shop, and then returned home to put up their Christmas tree. Dwayne popped the question after placing the final trimmings on their newly decorated tree. The ring was the final ornament!

Planning their wedding was a great experience that Dwayne and Karl will both cherish for a lifetime, and they learnt so many new things about one another in the process.

When asked about the inspiration for their day, the grooms-to-be wanted everyone to walk in and immediately know that it was THEIR wedding. They blocked out the noise of others' opinions and decided on a moody, minimalist and masculine look that was fueled by purposeful thoughts and ideas.

Choosing outfits was a personal process that was different for both men. Dwayne changed his look three times in the lead up! On the other hand, Karl's choice was much easier, as he selected a "classic" look, an all black tuxedo, white tuxedo shirt and white bow tie.

The couple delved into several DIY projects, including creating a decal for their tongue-in-cheek wedding sign which stated, "Choose a seat not a side, we're all family once the knot is tied!"

On the morning of their big day they started off with breakfast at their hotel: the infamous Hotel Monaco, which they said was "the perfect way to decompress and prepare our minds for the day ahead." They then went and got fresh haircuts from their barber and returned to their hotel to get ready together.

Their photographers Corinne Thompson and second shooter Alicia Wiley arrived and started an afternoon of photo-taking across various backdrops before the ceremony began.

As promised, their ceremony began at 5:30 pm (5+3=8 and 8 equals new beginnings) and it was exactly what they imagined it would be! Their vows were officiated by Rev. Laura Cannon who performed a magical ceremony tailor-made just for them. During the ceremony, Dwayne and Karl purposely had their guests seated in a circular design around them, because they wanted to be surrounded by love.

Then guests enjoyed a dream cocktail hour featuring many of the newlywed's favourites. Cue: endless fresh pizza, bacon treats, donut burgers and their signature cocktail: a watermelon jalapeno margarita!

During the cocktail hour, the couple escaped for a memorable moment alone to exhale and take in everything that had just happened.

After switching into their custom Converse Chuck Taylor sneakers, the newlyweds joined their guests at the reception for a wonderful night of toasts, dinner, dancing, cake and laughter. There really couldn't have been a more perfect ending.

Photography
Love to the Core Photo

Florals
Love and Luster

Food
Copper Kitchen MD

Hair
Melvin Miles

Jewelry
David Yurman

Menswear
Nordstrom, Bonobos

Music
Morgan State Band, Michele Fowlin, MyDeeJay

Officiant
Ceremony Officiants

Planning
Tira Lynn Events

Rentals
Select Event Group, White Glove Rentals, Event Dynamics Inc

Venue
Mt. Washington Mill Dye House

Why can't men hold bouquets?
HOW TO MAKE YOUR WEDDING MORE GENDER-NEUTRAL

ONE
HAVE AN INCLUSIVE WEDDING PARTY

There is no reason why that wedding party of yours can't be made up of different genders - if they're the important people in your life that you couldn't imagine marrying your best friend without, their gender should not stop that.

TWO
ADDRESS YOUR INVITES INCLUSIVELY

This one is super simple - just use names on your invitations instead of addressing 'Mr, Ms, Mx, etc.' We'd suggest popping the names on the invites in alphabetical order - super inclusive.

THREE
FORGET GENDERED PRE-WEDDING EVENTS

A hens night for just the ladies, a bucks party for just the boys - boring! There's a pretty high chance your favorite people are of mixed genders, so the parties you throw before the main event should be the same.

Need a more inclusive name for your pre-wedding party? Just throw a bach party, or an 'I'm getting married' celebration!

FOUR
HAVE FLORALS FOR EVERYONE; WHY CAN'T MEN HOLD BOUQUETS TOO?

Florals are for everyone, and wedding florals don't just have to be in a bouquet. Sure, you could have a floral boutonniere, but you could also have florals in the hair (including beards) or florals attached to your attire creatively, like over the shoulder.

FIVE
DON'T MAKE THE WEDDING PARTY PARTNER UP

You know that awkward tradition of partnering up someone from each side of the wedding party to walk down the aisle together - just have your wedding party walk down together as a group, as individuals, or another creative way.

SIX
STOP WITH THE GENDERED LANGUAGE

Bridal party, bridal suite, etc, it is an old school thing to make weddings all about the 'bride.' It's super easy to use non-gendered language like 'wedding party' and 'wedding suite' for these things.

Photography by Emma Weiss

SEVEN

ASK YOUR WEDDING PROS TO USE GENDER-NEUTRAL LANGUAGE

This one is especially true for those whose vendors are going to be there with you on the day. Ask your wedding vendors to use gender-neutral language for your guests - it is a good reminder that pronouns can't be assumed.

EIGHT

DON'T ADDRESS THE ROOM AS LADIES AND GENTLEMEN

...because there might not just be ladies and gentlemen in the room - the employed people who are working your wedding night included. 'Friends and Family' or something as simple as 'Hey, Everyone' also works as an all-inclusive option.

NINE

PUT PRONOUNS ON PLACECARDS

You could ask your guests for their pronouns when they are RSVP'ing to your wedding day. Print those pronouns on place cards. This will especially make it easy for guests who haven't yet grasped asking new people for their pronouns and create a warm and inviting space for your gender diverse guests.

TEN

HAVE GENDER-NEUTRAL BATHROOMS

We still can't understand why gender-specific bathrooms are important, especially at an event like a wedding. Ask your venue to remove any gendered signage, or cover it up with something you have created.

ELEVEN

DANCE WITH WHOEVER YOU WANT TO DANCE WITH

It might be a tradition for men to have their first dance with their mothers, and women with their fathers, but we say throw that tradition right out the window and dance with whoever you want to dance with.

Maybe you only want a first dance with your new spouse; maybe you don't want to dance at all. You do you, whatever feels right.

SAUSALITO, UNITED STATES OF AMERICA

JAY & JENNA

PHOTOGRAPHY BY EVE ROX PHOTOGRAPHY
www.everoxphotography.com

After ditching their fantasy of a rad do-it-yourself wedding day in an empty warehouse because it was way too much work, Jay and Jenna found their perfect venue and unleashed a theme that was appropriately and hilariously characterized as 'Earth Tones meets My Little Pony.'

Jay and Jenna met as roommates in an awesome apartment, near Dolores Park. However, after starting to date and deciding to give love a shot, they ditched the apartment in a move that they say was 100% worth it.

The couple eventually made a home together in New York but were back visiting San Francisco. They found themselves on a reminiscent walk through Dolores Park. Jay had sneakily hid a diamond ring at the bottom of a Bi-Rite ice-cream cone that Jenna was eating. When Jenna reached the ring, Jay got down on one knee and surprised her with his proposal.

Both Jay and Jenna have strong aesthetics, so, at their convergence... the 'Earth Tone/ My Little Pony' theme just naturally arose. The couple loved that when it all came together on the day; it was romantic, colourful, surreal, and fun all-in-one.

They found it super empowering to appropriate the hetro-normative tradition of marriage by personalizing it to make their ideal day, in every possible way. They gave themselves the leeway to embrace the mindset of rejecting any requirements or expectations that were motivated by anything other than their love story.

Their wedding day was totally unique, but totally Jay and Jenna.

Choosing outfits, was something they admit was tough for them both. Jenna's first dress was a complete disaster that ended up being returned after many re-fittings and lots of tears. She found her final dress only three weeks before their wedding date.

Jay knew they wanted to ride the line between modern and classic. After trying on the tuxedo jacket at Suit Supply, they knew they had their look and everything else fell in to place.

On their wedding day, Jay and Jenna recall a favorite moment: driving over the Golden Gate bridge to their venue, The Headlands Center for the Arts. This was the moment when it all started to feel real.

With the support of their co-officiants—a dear friend and their future brother-in-law, Jay and Jenna drew on queer history and Jewish tradition to write their ceremony. This created a ceremony that was extremely personal and connected to their roots.

Another moment that the newlyweds recall as being one of the funnest of the day, was during the champagne toast, when they got to see all their guests together in one place for the first time.

When asked about what marriage means to them, their first response was 'Gay-AF!'

Their wedding day gave them the chance to make every detail of the day their own. They believe that through collective power, the creative spirit that the queer community brings to marriage, can evolve the meaning of an oppressive tradition and make the world a better place.

Jay and Jenna are happy, living their best cosy lives in committed bliss, and for them, it doesn't get any better than that.

"We took on two big DIY projects before the wedding day.

Jay, and a couple of friends including a ceramacist, (Founder of Jo Boyer Ceramics) hand made pinch pots that served as incense burners in our favor bags.

Jay stuffed all the favor bags with the bowls, palo santo and cedar stick incense gifted from friends at Ritual Incense. Jenna created informative intention cards to go along with the gift bags.

We also had a napkin dying party where we dyed all of our flour-sack napkins with friends in the back yard. Both were tons of work but made the day more memorable and meaningful to us."

Photographer
Eve Rox Photography

Cake
Miette

Catering
Katie Powers Catering

Event Planner
Partial Planning by Heartthrob Weddings

Florist
Tropic of Flowers

Gown
Essence of Australia

Hair & Makeup
Elizabeth Windust, Love and Wolves Beauty

Jacket & Pants
Suit Supply

Lighting & Sound
Marin Lighting + JK Sound

Photo Booth
Photomatica

Signage & Stationery
Mike Wilcox, Tropic of Flowers

Wedding Rings
Esquelito

Venue
Headlands Center for the Arts

INTRODUCING

Shane Ave.

Who is Shane Ave?
Shane Ave is a journey to freedom of expression!

We are a non-gender formal attire company that prides itself on being able to provide a safe, friendly and comfortable environment for everyone to be able to validate their identity without judgment when choosing formal attire.

As someone who is a part of the community, I recognized the hole in the market and set out to fill it with a brand and company that allows all queers to feel confident, validated and understood without judgment or fear.

And, why were you inspired to do what you do?
Witnessing the elation and happiness in our clients is the driving force for us!

Suits, pants, vests, and shirts are a staple in all queer wardrobes, yet resources for lesbians, transmen and non-binary persons to buy a suit or shirt that actually fits and feels amazing are almost non-existent.

We know that formal fashion in general terms is very gender-specific and often doesn't allow the freedom of expressing one's own identity.

We noticed that LGBTQ+ people specifically are left out in the market place and that the community had nowhere to go that allows them to feel confident and comfortable to purchase their chosen formal attire.

Shane Ave was born out of a need to provide formal fashion that blurs traditional lines of gender divisions. There has been a very big hole in the market for too long.

We want everyone to feel safe to take a journey with Shane Ave in the knowledge that this is your journey, your style and your opportunity to be free, to validate and affirm your own identity with confidence and freedom.

We are passionate about giving everybody the opportunity to feel empowered, confident and comfortable when they walk out the door.

Are suits for every body?
Yes, most definitely!

At Shane Ave, we aim to design and create a style that suits every client regardless of their identity or style.

We cater to butch masculine, femme, softbutch, gay, transmen, transwomen and every person in between. We also welcome our allys to the LGBTQ+ community, of any gender, who want a great custom made suit that is designed especially for them - if you want to wear a suit, a suit is for you.

Size and style is no barrier with all our suits because each and every one is made to measure.

Check out our website or social media pages for some awesome inspiration in styles and designs.

What does the process of a custom Shane Ave suit look like?
The process can be done in a number of ways.

We offer face to face consultations in our flagship store in Sydney, and at our pop up stores that happen across Australia. We visit every state in Australia 3 times per year and we're starting these consultations over in the US in 2020.

These consultations take about 1hr and all styling, designing, and measurements are included in the process by either myself or one of our qualified stylists.

Or, we offer Skype and Facetime consultations for those who can't make it to a one-on-one consultation.

During these consultations, we guide the client through the styling and fabric selection process however the measurements are completed by the client using our unique measurement guide which includes a video tutorial.

And, if the idea of a consultation doesn't entice you, there's an opportunity to grab your suit off the shelf online.

We've tried our best to make this process as seamless as possible. Clients can choose all their own fabrics, styles and designs. And, like we mentioned there is a measurement guide, complete with video tutorials to guide you.

Do you only sell custom pieces, and do you ship around the world?
At this stage all our pieces are made to measure however we will be launching an off the rack range of shirts and t-shirts early 2020 with plans to launch a jacket and pants off the rack range later in the year. The best news though is that we ship all around the world!

Do you have any suggestions for people, who struggle with their body in some way or another, on how to relieve their worries around fittings?
We are fast becoming the name on everyone's lips when it comes to formal attire whether that be for weddings, social engagements or work.

Photography by Alana Taylor Photography

Apart from the fact we provide high quality and professional craftsmanship in all our pieces, feedback from clients tells us that the success and rapid growth of Shane Ave is largely because of the safe and comfortable environment we provide for everyone.

All measurements are taken fully clothed which offers our clients that may struggle with their body in one way or another, to feel completely comfortable.

It is our passion and promise to everyone, to ensure a safe and comfortable environment when choosing their formal attire. It's something that every person deserves, especially when they are finding an outfit for a special occassion, like their wedding day!

Tell us more about your podcast, The Unsuitable.
The Unsuitable is a natural extension of the business, presenting the stories of some of the world's most interesting people in the queer community, that we have had the opportunity to meet through Shane Ave.

When clients come for a consultation they will often share their stories, some are quite harrowing and confronting whilst others are warm and heart filling.

The more stories I heard the more inspired I was to tell the world these stories and help our LGBTQ+ community and the wider community to gain some insight and better understanding of people in the queer community.

What's next for Shane Ave?
After an incredible reception at New York Fashion week last year, Shane Ave will be launching in the United States later this year with two consultants already secured in Atlanta and Chicago. It's an expansion that we are so thrilled about.

We will also be appointing consultants in every state of Australia to be available for consultations all year-round instead of just a few times a year.

We will be taking our pop-up store to New Zealand in April, which is a first and we are very excited about that.

We look forward to bringing the off the rack lines to fruition and continuing to serve the queer community.

TORONTO, CANADA

IAN & STEPHEN

PHOTOGRAPHY BY BOWS AND LAVENDER
www.bowsandlavender.com

"Neither of our families had ever attended a 'gay wedding' before, so there was definitely a level of anticipation and pressure we felt to make sure it lived up to expectations.

In the beginning, we struggled with which 'traditional' elements we wanted to incorporate, which would be expected of us, and which we felt didn't necessarily 'fit' what we thought a 'gay wedding' meant to us.

In the end, we decided that staying true to us and our story was more important than anyone else's expectations, and that's kind of what we used to guide our decisions.

As it turns out, that's what everyone was expecting anyway!"

Yin and Yang lovebirds, Ian and Stephen, met at a house party over 10 years ago when they were both dating other people. Those relationships soon fizzled out and it was clear to them both, that there was something worth exploring with each other. And... the rest is history!

Seven years later, they set off for their annual trip with friends to Prince Edward County for a weekend of wine and debauchery. Little did Stephen know, that Ian was planning an epic proposal.

While touring the vineyard, Ian slipped away for a bathroom break whilst an unassuming Stephen continued the tour with their friends (who all knew what was about to happen). When they reached the barrelling building, the doors opened to reveal Ian surrounded by candles and string lights, down on one knee. The proposal was one of the happiest moments of their lives, and of course, Stephen said "Yes!"

After an initial struggle choosing their wedding theme and which 'traditional' elements they wanted to incorporate, they decided that staying true to themselves was important to them.

As a result, the initial direction Stephen gave to their visual team, Index Creative, was 'part Britney Spears 'My Perogative' music video, part Met Gala- but make it us!' They wanted a chic, but moody party vibe that really invited their guests to let loose and celebrate!

Although they collaborated with a lot of their friends in the planning process, they do admit to creating their very own 'Wedding Bible'. This was basically a 35-page long, complete brand guide for their wedding, detailing every aspect to ensure everyone was on the same page about every detail.

To fit in with their neutral colour palette for the wedding (mainly black, white, greys and champagne tones) they dressed their wedding parties in black tux's and champagne dresses. To make sure they stood out, the grooms' tuxedos had black slacks and white jackets to give them an extra slick pop!

On the morning of their wedding they drank champagne and laughed as they both separately practiced their vows on their closest friends, and slowly got themselves groomed for the event.

Photographer, Bows and Lavender whisked the grooms-to-be away, a few hours before their ceremony to do a 'first look' shoot in their tuxedos. The shoot took place in an alley-way across from the hotel, and those photos did not disappoint!

In a sea of nerves and excitement, they then headed to Berkeley Church for their ceremony.

They both say that the moment their eyes met was so emotional and they found it hard not to tear up. The entire church stood up and started clapping as the grooms met in the middle of the aisle and walked down it together. It was pure magic!

The newlyweds and their guests then buckled in for a night of live music, food, speeches and performances, that they say, were all... absolutely perfect.

Ian and Stephen had felt committed for a long time, but say having a wedding became a great reason to celebrate their love. Their union also serves as the most powerful reminder of how much love and support they are surrounded by in their everyday lives.

Photographer
Bows and Lavender

Cake
Glory Hole Doughnuts

Catering
Berkeley Church

Decorative Elements
Index Creative

Engagement Rings
Tiffany & Co.

Entertainment
Tynomi Banks, DJ Phil Villeneuve

Event Stylist
Index Creative

Suit Designer
Rented from Andrews Formals

Venue
Berkeley Church

Say goodbye to boring, plain or generic ties and bowties, and a give a very enthusiastic welcome to bright and bold prints created exclusively for the label by Australian designers.

Peggy and Finn have arrived to the party!

We adore these original prints, they pack a punch in all the right ways. Sure to make a real statement. Often inspired by botanicals there is something for every personality. Also, they've expanded into socks and undies too, and have an adorable kids collection - swoon.

www.peggyandfinn.com

Melbourne based artist, Francis Cannon has teamed up with Third Draw Down to bring to life a fun collection that looks at ideas of body-love, body-loathing, anxiety, relationships, sex, sexuality, gender and bodily functions - just a handful of our favorite things!

We are head over heels for every piece but the 'Franny Pack' is the real show stopper.

www.thirddrawerdown.com

We are huge, like really huge, fans of confetti - but we hate, like really hate, the environmental impact confetti can have. Plus, you'll find a whole head of wedding venues will have pretty strict rules when it comes to this very topic.

If handmade biodegradable, earth-friendly, confetti made with love is on your wedding 'need' list, you'll need to check out Eco Confetti. Good for the earth and looks incredible in photos - a guilt-free 'we're married celebration' confetti.

www.econfetti.com.au

THINGS WE LOVE

If you're on the hunt for some inclusive wedding stationery that celebrates your love, meet, Two Brides Presents.

Their stationery offers a diverse range of pre-designed styles created by independent Australian Artists which can be personalized on so many levels. If you are after a truly original design, the team are also pros at creating something custom, totally unique. Packages are tailored to suit your big day and your budget. They also offer some adorable inclusive cards for other important events like birthdays and engagements.

www.twobridespresents.com

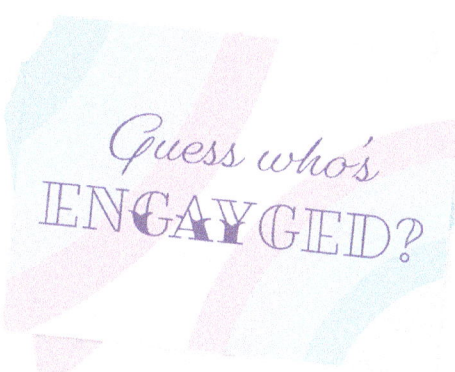

We don't want to alarm you, but, we've found an incredible handmade shoe brand that doesn't gender there shoes. As in, the designs, like our favourite Plain Plaid Toe shoes above, are available in a huge selection of sizes. So, if you're a smaller footed person you don't need to miss out on your favorite designs.

Parallel Shoes is a brand based in America, but they ship to lovers across the globe.

www.parallelshoes.com

WIN

Want to have this little ring all for yourself (or to gift to someone you really love?) We're giving away a 9ct yellow gold crater ring, with a sparkling diamond, handcrafted by Albert Tse Metalsmith.

Competition is open to lovers across the world. You can enter via dancingwiththem.com/win

www.alberttsemetalsmith.com

ISAIAH + TAYLOR

Los Angeles Wedding Photographers

IsaiahAndTaylor.com

NEW YORK, UNITED STATES OF AMERICA

LAUREN & SAM

PHOTOGRAPHY BY ELVIRA KALVISTE
www.weddingsbyelvira.com

Brooklyn couple Lauren and Sam haven't always called New York home. In fact, the couple met in Texas in 2014 and lived all over the country before settling in their forever home.

Not only have they travelled their home country, but they have spent their time together having epic adventures all around the globe and making some of their favorite memories along the way.

For Sam, waking up in Lake Como with her partner was one of her fondest memories. She recalls looking over at Lauren, who had planned that stretch of the vacation, and was enamored with the life they get to live together. For Lauren, it was a trip to Greece with just the two of them out on a balcony, soaking up the sun and making each other laugh.

The couple got engaged the weekend after the US Presidential Election in 2016. Like much of America, they were shell-shocked when Trump won and they were very unsure of what the future would hold for gay rights, trans rights, and the right to marry. When they started dating, they couldn't legally get married, so they decided to lock it down while they were under Obama's Presidency, out of principle more than anything else. With about two months to plan, they set their wedding date for January 7, 2017... two weeks before Trump would be officially inaugurated.

So, with a small guest list that included their Californian and Texan family members, amidst a massive snow storm, the couple tied the knot in an artist loft in Williamsburg.

The loft was like a warm haven from the frozen outside world. Fifty of their closest friends and family surrounded them and witnessed their vows. It was intimate, candlelit, with minimal decor or fuss- just them, committing to each other.

Though Lauren and Sam are now a happily married couple that are both content with their own identities and relationship nuances, gay marriage rights have not been the only gender based obstacle that they have had to overcome.

Lauren was about six months into her outward transition when she met Sam; she was also leaving behind a marriage that didn't honor her gender expression. Sam was 23 and just making her emergence from inside the closet.

When Lauren told Sam that she is transgender, they didn't know what to think at first. Sam told her "I've got a lot of questions, but I'd love to know more about your journey." This resulted in Lauren truly opening her eyes and ears to a whole new language surrounding gender, identity and expression. The questions that this new knowledge arose, brought about revelations that were working on Sam from the inside out. They started feeling the lightbulb come on, like they finally understood why they never belonged with the 'girls.'

It took them about five years to come to the realization that they are non-binary and even then, it wasn't until they saw themselves on television (the couple were part of a show called Couples Therapy on Showtime), that they realized they didn't want to continue showing themself to the world as a woman. They were obsessing over the idea that they didn't look like themself on the show- like they were dressed in a costume. And those little inklings, combined with many years of thinking through gender identity with Lauren, helped them to come out as non-binary and change their name to something that felt truer to them.

Lauren, who has seen the gender variances in Sam since day one and has been so patient and kind in waiting for them to fully accept themself, has been nothing but supportive of their identity transformation. In fact, she was so excited to see them step out into the light of who they really are!

Sam says if there were any signs of tension, it was that Lauren was pushing them to accept their truest self before they were completely ready. Sam now has a better understanding of their own gender-dysphoria triggers and can now better empathize with Lauren, about what she has gone through for so long.

Being in an open relationship is also something that is important to them, because the goal within their partnership is to never limit each other or themselves. It was very early on in their relationship (third date to be exact!) that Sam told Lauren that they didn't see cheating as an option or a reason for them to ever break up. It was their young way of saying "I don't expect you to never be sexually attracted to other people, so let's be real about that up front." Sam believes that when monogamy is assumed and

never discussed, it can give unrealistic expectations about themselves and each other. They officially started seeing other people about six months after their wedding. They were cautious at first and started out with some ground rules, that have slowly melted away as they've built this specific form of trust with one another. They don't always date other people, in fact it's rare. However, they've found the experience to be mind-opening, whilst also providing them with the feeling of being free, autonomous people in the context of a committed marriage.

One of the biggest challenges they have faced in their relationship has been deconstructing heteronormative power imbalances. As queer people, Lauren and Sam sometimes feel that they may have side-stepped the trappings of daily social constructs; such as their individual relationships to money and how rooted they are in patriarchy and antiquated gender norms... but say if they look closely enough, they are definitely there. Woven into the fabric of their childhood and societal conditionings, they have different ideas about how to relate to money and how they think about child rearing and timeline, etc.

Nonetheless, they do their best to take these challenges as moments of growth and say they have learnt so much from each other on these topics, but at times it hasn't been easy!

When asked about what advice they can offer other couples going through similar subjects, staying honest and communicative was top of the list. Keeping lines free and open and not being afraid to tell each other what you truly want or how you really feel about everything. Finally, treating your relationship like you're a team is a great way to get aligned, know what you want to accomplish in your relationship and design the world you want to live in... together!

Lauren and Sam now have some big dreams ahead of them- dreams of a boutique interior design company, furniture flipping, eventually working on films together and adding children into their family unit.

They both agree, that they're pumped up about all of it!

RUSTED VASE
—— FLORAL CO. ——

Photos by Sergio Alcala Photography

Flowers For The Wildly Romantic
- Wild, Unique, and Wandering -

www.rustedvase.com

Breaking Traditions

HOW THESE LGBTQ+ COUPLES TOOK WEDDING TRADITIONS AND MADE THEM THEIR OWN

Andrew & Martin

Our proposal wasn't a secret to either of us, rather a mutual decision that we discussed at length. We forego any real 'traditional' engagement, and instead, we started making wedding plans after that discussion - no rings exchanged.

Martin, being a little more impatient than Andrew, did go about buying the wedding bands himself and used them to 'propose' to Martin a few weeks after that initial decision. It was more a romantic gesture than anything else.

Kelsey & Lina

Conscious of the environmental impact of diamonds (and metals), Lina had a ring handcrafted from recycled metals and had a sapphire from her Grandmothers engagement ring set as a feature stone.

It's a repurposed ring that has a lot of sentimental value. One that Kelsey wears so proudly.

Kegan & Tag

Tag works as a medical professional, and so when they are at work, a ring is out of the question - and, to be quite frank, Tag has never been a 'ring' person.

Kegan proposed, in place of any sort of engagement ring, with a beautiful watch. On the back of the watch, Kegan had the date that we first met engraved. The day our lives forever changed.

Sarah & Yara

In day to day life we work hard to reduce our environmental impact, our engagement and our wedding will be no different. Sarah actually found an Etsy seller who created rings from recycled skateboards.

It's an accidental nod to the beginnings of our relationship where we Yara would spend hours trying to teach Sarah how to board, with not a lot of success.

Sarah got down on one knee with the 'non-traditional' ring and Yara couldn't have been any quicker to say 'yes!'

Dane & Ryan

Dane actually proposed with a tattoo! You wouldn't consider either of us shy when it comes to getting new ink. Dane actually booked us in for a couples tattoo session, something that we had done before, so Ryan was unsuspecting.

He planned a wonderful lunch where we talked all things our future, what we envisioned a life together would look like, and even our journey to parenthood. Dane very sweetly asked during the lunch 'will you marry me?', Ryan of course answering 'yes'. The matching tattoos signify that commitment to one another.

A Diamond Engagement Ring

Photography by Marylane Photography

Walking Down the Aisle

Dylan & Robert

We didn't have an aisle at all! We only ever wanted a small wedding and had just 37 guests present on the day. We had a private first look with our photographer before heading to our venue together. We arrived before our guests and so had the opportunity to greet them all as they arrived.

When the time came to get married, our officiant (and dear friend) called for our guests to be seated, and we casually made our way to the front of the area as they settled.

No grand entrance required. It was authentic to us.

Abbey & Kim

We didn't even think about who would walk down the aisle first until our celebrant reached out to confirm about a week before the wedding - talk about being chilled out brides!

After we laughed at our own lack of organization, we decided that it would be fun to toss a coin on the day.

We got ready together, made our way to the venue as a team, and at the top of the aisle, we tossed the coin. Kim chose heads, and she walked first - escorted by both her Mom and Dad. Abbey followed with her proud older brother on her arm.

Sure, it wasn't a 'traditional' way to go about it, but it definitely got a laugh from our loved ones!

Bobby & Julie

Since the beginning of our relationship, we have seen one another as equal. The tradition of walking down the aisle and being 'given away' by our parents was something that just didn't sit well with us.

So, we decided to walk down that aisle, and into the next chapter of our lives, together. Hand in hand, it felt like we drifted down the aisle in an emotional, almost dream-like, state.

Stacey & Yumi

We consciously decided to find a venue that would allow us to both walk down the aisle, separately. It wasn't an easy task, but with a creative stylist on board, it came to life.

Our venue had space that allowed us to both walk down two different aisles, toward one other. It really allowed us to be in the moment; eyes locked on one another from the minute 'our song' started to play. We both remember the moment as one filled with pride and joy - the pre-ceremony anxiety dissipated almost instantly.

Grant & Augie

We eloped, so technically, there wasn't an aisle!

Photography by Sara Hannagan Photography

The Wedding Party

Dylan & Robert

We are social butterflies and with a guest list just shy of 200, our wedding party was just as grand - seven on each side. Each of us had our siblings and a handful of friends, a wedding party of both men and women.

We did set rules around what we wanted the wedding party to wear. We wanted to stick to a neutral color palette for our beach wedding. Our groomsmen did wear matching, hired, sand-colored suits, however, the women of our wedding party wore dresses that they chose themselves. We wanted them to feel comfortable and wear a dress that they could wear again!

Alex & Roberta

Choosing a wedding party was really tough for us! Initially we shortlisted people that we thought we would like to stand beside us. However, we were planning an intimate wedding, and eventually, we came to the conclusion that we didn't really need a wedding party at all.

Instead, we decided to invite those people closest to us to get ready with us. And, when the time came to make our way to our ceremony, we all caught a bus together for the grand entrance!

Bobbi & Mandy

In planning our entire wedding there was never any conformity to old school traditions, and mapping out our wedding party was no different! Bobbi had three people that they wanted beside them, and Mandy had six. So, we had misnumbered wedding parties! We also knew that we wanted every person standing beside us to feel comfortable, confident and beautiful. And so, we decided that everyone in our wedding parties could choose what they wanted wear.

It was a mix of colors, dresses, suits, jumpsuits and it could not have been any more perfect! We think the smiles on everyone's faces says it all.

Alex & Arnold

We actually have a large joint friend group, and so we found that when we started discussing the wedding party, we realized that there was some crossover! Obviously, when thinking about where they would stand, there were some logistical issues.

We eventually decided that our wedding party would be a joint wedding party! We got ready in separate rooms, our people moving between the two of us. They walked, very enthusiastically, down the aisle just before us, and all nine of them took their seats front and center at the ceremony.

Then at the reception, they all sat with us on a shared table. It was an awesome way to have them all involved in our love celebration.

Photography by Studio XIII Photography

Dean & Nigel

Dean proposed first, but Nigel proposed back, asking Dean, 'can I be the man to take your last name?'

Nigel has two older brothers who have carried on the family name, and keeping his last name just wasn't important.

He officially took on the new last name about six months after we were married.

Casey & Eleven

It took us a long time to decide what we would do about surnames after our marriage. Neither of us felt emotionally connected to our 'family name.' We spoke about hyphenating, or not changing them at all, but anticipating children for our future, we wanted to have a name that represented our family unit.

We actually ended up deciding that we would choose our own new surname. We are avid outdoor enthusiasts, and we planned our a 'proposal hike' with the intention that we would both have a chance to propose at some point during the hike.

That mountain is a special place for us; it is where we declared our commitment to one another. And so, its name was a natural choice for our own new family name, Rainier.

Amy & LeAndra

We are both career-driven women and have worked hard to build our professional profiles. We never found ourselves having a discussion over the whole 'changing your last name' tradition. Instead, it was assumed that we would both keep our last names - personally and professionally. It's also something that neither of us found importance in, it seemed like an outdated tradition we just weren't interested in fulfilling.

We were taken back by just how many questions our family would ask about the decision, particularly questions around what we would do if we chose to expand our family. Although we don't know exactly what we will do (it is still a few years away, if it will ever happen), we both agree that we might go down the road of hyphenating our child's last name.

Marc & Sam

We went back and forth on what to do with our surnames for our entire engagement and during the first few months of marriage.

We eventually decided that hyphenating our two names was the best choice for us. We wanted to have a unifying surname (we dreamt of a sign at the front of our farm, proudly displaying our family name), but it didn't feel right for either of us to give up the meaningful names we've carried with us through life.

Photography by Maria Luise Bauer Photography

TEN YEARS OF MARRIAGE

MATT & ZAC

PHOTOGRAPHY BY MARISSA SOLINI PHOTOGRAPHY
www.marissasolini.com

Love grows and shifts during a long-term relationship. Matt and Zach have been together more than 15 years, and married for 10. Their lives have intertwined, they have grown together, and their love is just as strong as ever.

How did you two meet?
Z: We met on the first Wednesday of September 2004 at a gay bar in Providence, Rhode Island, called Mirabar. Matt went to Brown University and I went to the University of Rhode Island. We seem to remember it was college night at the bar during the week that everyone was moving onto their respective campuses.

We were both there with friends, and I was there to dance it all out before classes started the following week. Matt came up to dance with me and tried to chat over the ear-damagingly loud music.

Before he left for the night, he asked for my number, but he had no cell phone to type it into (these were still early cell phone days), nor anything to write with. So, I typed my number into my own phone and he memorized the number.

He called me a week later for a date and we dated almost weekly that fall.

How long have you two been together? And when was your wedding?
M & Z: We met over 15 years ago! We got married on October 9, 2009, in Massachusetts, where Matt is from and where same-sex marriage had been tried and tested for five years. Legality was still patchwork throughout the states then, and only domestic partnership was available in Oregon where we lived, but, it all worked out for us to go back to the East Coast where we're both from and have our wedding there.

How did you two become engaged?
Z: I never cared if I married or not. At the time, it was not an option for me anyway. Also, I didn't have examples of happy, long-lasting marriages in my life and some of the most well-adjusted couples I knew, had been together for many years without ever getting married.

Matt had it in his mind that he would get married after he had reached certain milestones. At the age of 27, he had met all of those milestones.

One night in bed, before we had fallen asleep, he casually asked me if I thought we should get married. I knew that married or not, I could see myself with him for many, many years.

So, I said if it was important to him to get married, I would absolutely marry him.

Nothing fancy, but totally us.

When did each of you know you were in love with the other?
Z: In 2006, the year that I graduated, we got to spend a lot more time together in the months before graduation because I lived the closest I had ever lived to Matt up to that point.

I also knew that earlier that school year, I had made the decision to live in Oregon for a year to see if I liked it. If I decided I didn't, then I would move back to New England. Matt still had a year of school left, so I knew he couldn't come back west with me and that we would have to take a break or do a long-distance relationship. I didn't really want to do either, but knew that I could have ended up resenting Matt if I stayed for him instead of seeking something new.

I knew we really had something good and worth holding on to, when I was faced with the possibility that distance may cause it to slip from our hands or not.

M: About ten seconds before I asked him to marry me, I think.

I was doing a little prayer and meditation before bed, and I heard a voice this had happened one other time in my life. It told me to marry him. We'd always had such an easy connection, and I'd always felt like I was with the right person, without even being aware of that feeling.

I think that moment resulted from the realization that I was good enough to ask him to marry me.

What is your favorite quality about each other?
Z: I've learned from Matt that it is okay to make mistakes, and that perfection is not necessarily the best goal to keep in mind. That is not to say that he only makes mistakes; he just doesn't let the thought of mistakes or perfection hold him back as much as I feel it holds me back.

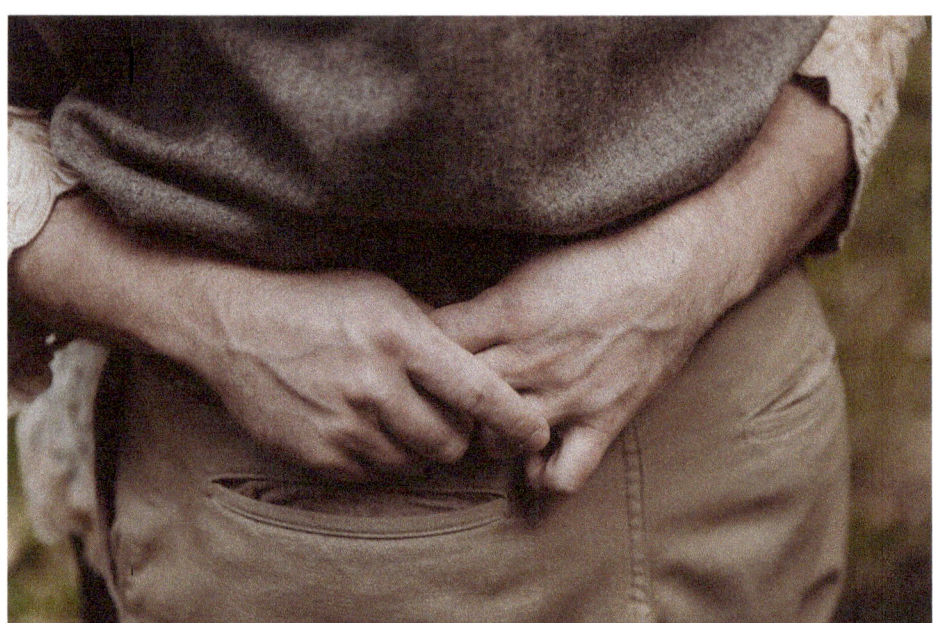

Being in a partnership with Matt has helped me push boundaries around this; something that I may not have explored without him.

M: Zach is extraordinarily considerate and just.

What are some of your favorite memories from your wedding day?

M: My most prominent memory is that of my grandmother, who was in the last stages of Alzheimer's, asking if I had any girlfriends or boyfriends, and her being very happy to learn she was at my wedding.

Z: I remember our families getting to meet for the first time. I remember nerves and laughter. I remember that it was threatening rain all morning, and we got married outside in a park, along a lakeshore down the street from Matt's parent's house.

I remember the awkwardness of standing in front of our families, so far apart, we couldn't even hold hands. I remember being very calm, but trying to smile because my calm face looks more severe.

I remember seeing nerves in Matt that I rarely see. We took a few photos after the ceremony, and as we drove up to the reception (a camp we had rented out for the weekend) that afternoon, the rain poured down!

How do you feel your love for each other has changed or grown over the years? Any advice you'd like to give couples for a long and happy marriage?
Z: Married life has its ups and downs, but so does a heart monitor, and if it is flat, you're in trouble.

Our culture focuses so much on how couples meet! I can't recall a single story or instance that focuses on how a couple stayed together through the years, or how they're doing seven years in - and that's a real shame.

There was a time about a year after we got married, when we both realized we could never be everything the other wanted or needed and that it was okay! That is a lot of pressure to put on someone, and we decided to take that pressure off of each other.

That was a very important realization!

We love to travel together, and those are the times that I have felt closest to Matt. He sets everything up with a direction and a general outline, and I work out details along the way. It's wonderfully collaborative.

When we aren't traveling, we fill our days with things that fulfill us individually, which means we sometimes don't see much of each other, but over the years, we have supported each other to grow and evolve.

We also love playing with our sweet adopted dog, Kirby.

We have become a safe home base for each other.

We check in with another about how things are going. We get to learn about each other's lives in a way that's exciting because we often share something new the other is hearing for the first time.

Sometimes that individualism catches up to us, and we find that we need to spend more quality time together, and that's often a nice change of pace.

It is all about the ebbs and flows.

AN ENGAGEMENT

LILY & OSCAR

PHOTOGRAPHY BY TUESDAY PHOTOGRAPHY
www.tuesdayphotography.com.au

Words by Oscar

We've been together for almost half a decade; it will be five years in July!

We had been best friends since we were 17, then I transitioned at 19, and we got together shortly after. We met at a mutual friend's house in the most simple way, and somehow it ended up being the most important meeting we both have ever had.

Lily was eager for a proposal, like, really, eager! I knew the only way to make her not think it was happening, was to make it seem like it really wasn't happening.

For six months, I let her believe that it wasn't important to me, and once I convinced her of that, she was so oblivious to everything I did regarding the proposal.

Lily didn't question why I was working so hard or pay attention to the money I was piling up, so all of that made keeping a secret pretty easy. No-one expects a big surprise if you tell them for six months that it's not going to happen!

I booked a holiday so that I could propose in a nice way, and since you do so many nice things on holiday, I knew she wouldn't expect it. The only issue with it was the added financial stress of getting an engagement ring and a holiday (overseas to the UK no less).

I was looking for a ring for two months before walking past a shop window and finding the perfect match, when I least expected it. Once I found that ring, I knew it was the only one that would come close to how beautiful she is.

I worked my ass off to get that ring for her, and it was so worth it! Then, I proposed to a very unsuspecting Lily on that holiday to the UK. It looked absolutely perfect on her, aside from the ring being the wrong size - something not simple to fix overseas.

When it comes to wedding planning, taking our time is most important to us since we don't want to add unnecessary stress. Some aspects of a "traditional" wedding can be nice, but a lot of it is so heteronormative.

We want to show our family that there is more to the queer world than a drag show!

We haven't planned the ins and outs of the day, but we do know we want our wedding filled with queer love, celebrations, and of course, wedding day outfits.

There hasn't been much planning done so far, but we do know that every guest is welcome to dress as binary or non-binary as they please.

Luckily enough, Lily's dad is an amazing florist, so flowers are sorted! Obviously, Tuesday Photography is our ideal choice for photos; we were absolutely in love with this shoot and we honestly don't think anyone could've captured our love any better.

We have so many friends who want to contribute to our wedding. Our friends have always been so supportive of our relationship, and it would be amazing to have them all involved in this celebration!

We are really trying to be individual with certain details and take inspiration from ourselves more than anything. Our biggest inspiration is, honestly, looking at a traditional wedding and doing the complete opposite of that!

"I think our engagement mostly just changed how other people see our relationship.

For me personally nothing changed, Oscar was always my life partner since the day I met him but the engagement just showed all our friends and family the realness of what we have.

Relationship wise no feelings changed, but from the outside there seems to be a lot of pressure to transform into full-fledged adults after the engagement and 'settle down'.

As much as I love that I'm spending my life with Oscar, we don't ever think that we could 'settle down'; that whole concept was birthed from het-culture.

We are deciding what this engagement and marriage is on our own terms, we are forever growing and changing, so 'settling down' isn't ever on the agenda."

Miss Tillie Walten
Kay
Tie
CAMPER REGISTRATION
FOR BRIDESMATES

festivities

Kay
Tie

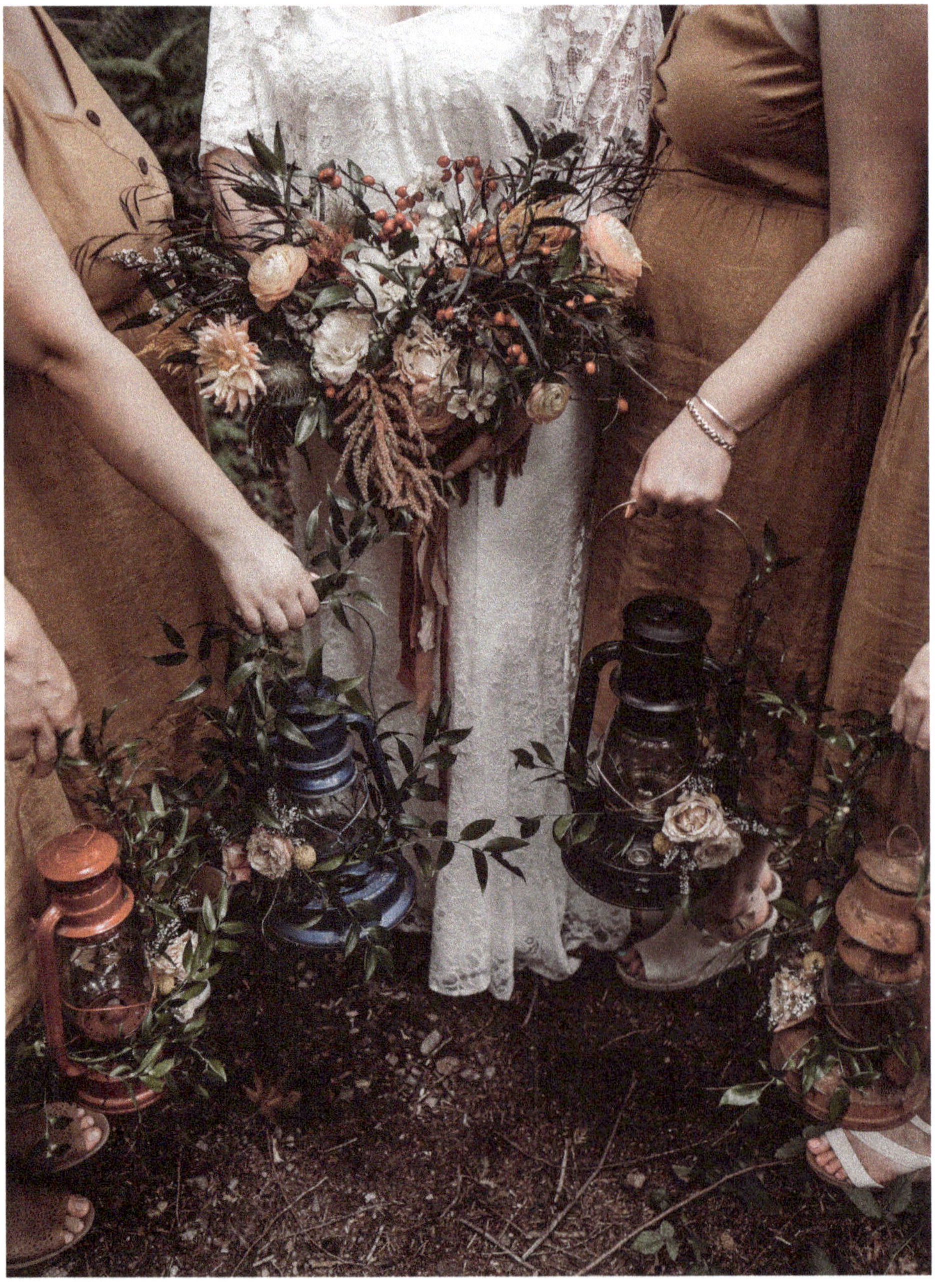

Catherine Anne & Kelci Kathleen
WALTEN
INVITE YOU TO SHARE
S'MORES WITH THEM
AT THEIR ONE-YEAR MARRIAGE BLESSING AND RELIGIOUS CEREMONY
AUGUST 31 - SEPTEMBER 2, 2019
WEDDING CEREMONY AT FIVE O'CLOCK IN THE EVENING ON SATURDAY, AUGUST 31
at Camp Huston
14725 LEY RD, GOLD BAR WA 98251

Tie
Kay

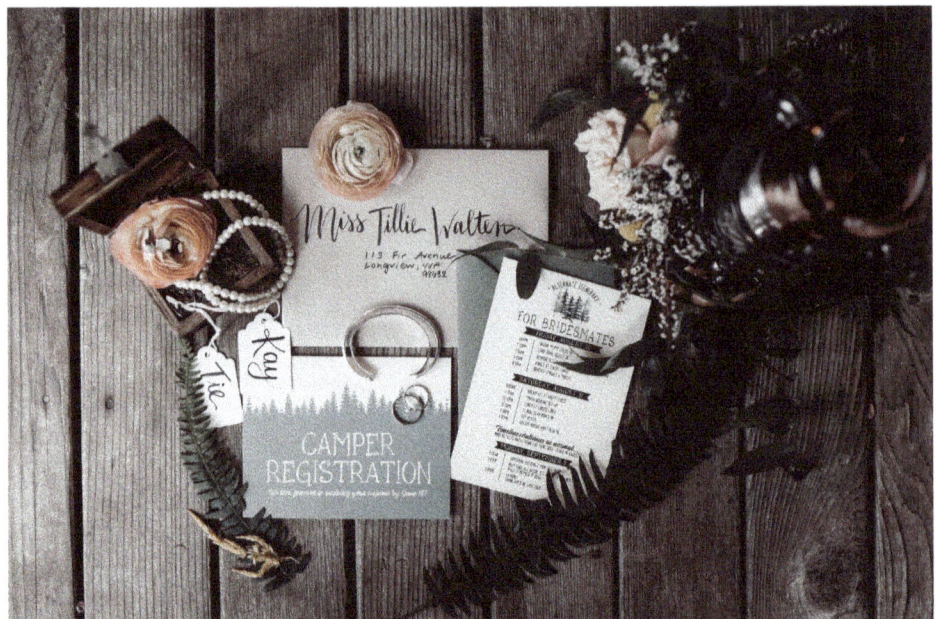

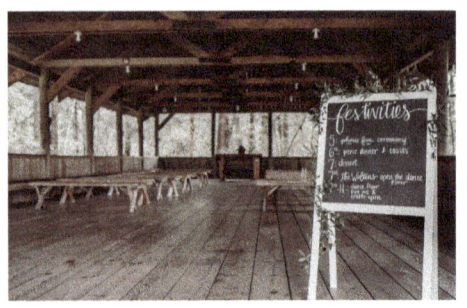

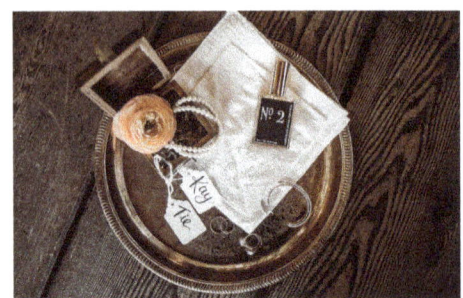

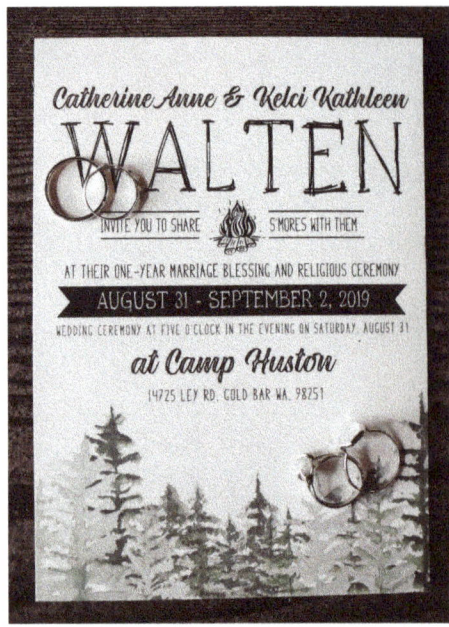

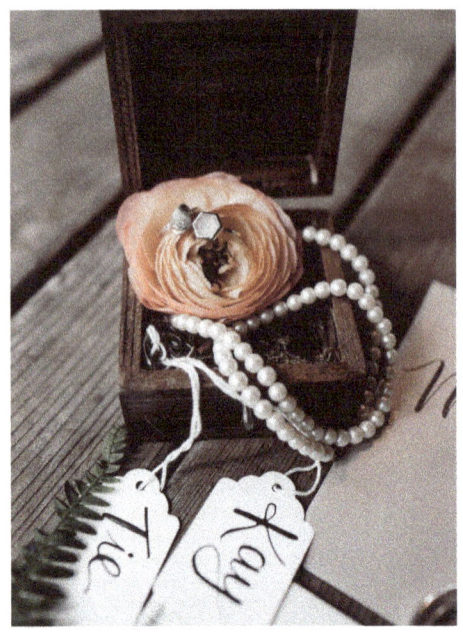

"I did a ton of DIY for our wedding!

I love to do projects for people, so getting to create things for our wedding was a huge act of love for Kay and our friends and family who would enjoy them with her.

I refurbished a custom s'mores table out of a torn up vintage vanity, learned to do calligraphy for all of our invites and signage, designed custom coloring books and goody bags for the kids coming to our wedding and handmade combination name tag place card buttons for each guest. It was quite an undertaking!

As a florist, I also did all of our floral design, which was my favorite gift to her. I cried the whole time I was making her floral belt because I knew she would walk down the aisle in it."

Kay and Katie had been half-jokingly proposing to one another for months. So much in fact, that when Kay proposed for real, it took Katie a moment to realise she was serious. Of course, she said "Yes!". Katie's proposal however, was much more elaborate.

As the couple were set to leave all their friends behind in Washington and move to Massachusetts, Katie wanted to plan a big do involving all their friends and family, so that they could see them off.

She created a scavenger hunt for Kay, taking her on a chronological journey of memorable places and events through their relationship. It involved lots of love letters, clues, family and spontaneous appearances of close friends... and then of course, a cliff-top proposal!

After their two unique and emotional proposals, Kay and Katie embarked on a carefully designed journey of creating a wedding event that was as sustainable as possible. Their whole wedding ending up being either thrifted, compostable or reusable in their lives.

They planned their theme based on their love of camping and the outdoors.

Their floral design was based around Kay's favorite greenery and included billy balls, evergreen trees, ferns, roses and ranunculus. For the flowers, they went with mustard tones and warm neutrals. They aimed to create a casual, intimate atmosphere where people could relax and enjoy the weekend's events.

Their venue, Camp Huston in Gold Bar, WA was chosen as Katie had gone their many times growing up. She took Kay there and experienced a perfect day (one of the most special in their entire lives).

They ended up sheltering from a surprise storm in the chapel, and spent at least an hour laying in the outdoor chapel talking about their future and families. It was perfect, and they knew it was the place for them!

Both women had trouble finding the perfect outfits. Kay found a lack of queer lady style icon to source inspo from, and Katie just found it hard to find anything that suited her sustainable ethos. In the end, they both found their perfect outfits with Katie settling on a perfect burgundy jumpsuit and Kay finding a gorgeous lace gown that she knows she'll wear again at some point.

On their wedding day, the brides-to-be recall some of their favourite moments being; helping each other get ready, their 'first look' with their brides-mates, walking down the aisle together, and when they rang the chapel bell after they kissed their bride!

Both Kay and Katie had different religious upbringings, but started the ceremony with a beautiful service of blessing and unity. They made sure that their bridal-family and parents were involved in some way. This included having their parents walk down the aisle, and playing their wedding songs at the reception, which was an absolute riot.

Their day was captured by Stacie from Widman Photography, who the brides say was just amazing. They honestly didn't remember her even being there in many moments, but somehow, she captured them! It meant for photographs are an authentic representation of the couples and their love.

Kay and Katie had the most beautiful wedding day, one that set the stage for the rest of their life together. A life of laughter, learning, growing, and changing with their best friend.

Photographer
Widman Photography

Cakes
Mama's Artisan Sweets, Bee's Custom Cakes

Catering
Randi and Jo Rolison, Bon Vivant

Ceremony Venue
St. John in the Woods Chapel

Cinematographer
Gavin Brown Media

Event Planner & Stylist
Blooms and Twine Floral Design (Bride Katie)

Florist
Blooms and Twine Floral Design (Bride Katie)

Gown Designer
Torrid

Jumpsuit Designer
Thrifted (Unknown)

Officiant
Rev. Josh Hosler, the Episcopal Church of the Good Shepherd

Reception Venue
Camp Huston

Rings
Dawn Vertrees Jewelry, HONED by Claire Kinder

INSPIRATION

RAINBOW LOVE

PHOTOGRAPHY BY HANNAH GILBERT PHOTOGRAPHY
www.hannahgilbert.com.au

Photography
Hannah Gilbert Photography

Florals & Styling
Pollen & Patina

Jewelry
Sally Rose Jewellery

Make-up
Elle James Makeup Artis

Props & Furniture Hire
Mewburn Park, Pollen & Patina

Shoes
UnDandy Shoes

Signage
Redpoint Design

Suits
Stobies Land & Surf

Ties
Peggy & Finn

Venue
Mewburn Park Homestead

YARRA VALLEY, AUSTRALIA

AB

PHOTOGRAPHY BY JAMES THORNE
www.jamesthorne.com.au

IMMERSE
YARRA VALLEY
RESTAURANT
RECEPTION
CELLAR DOOR

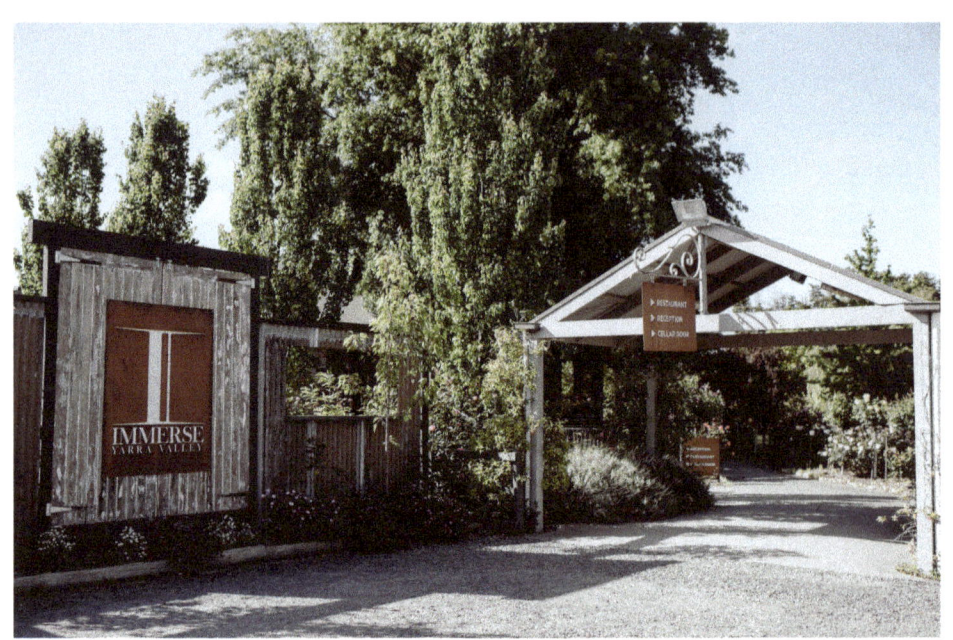

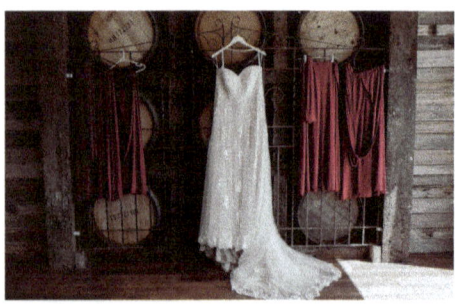

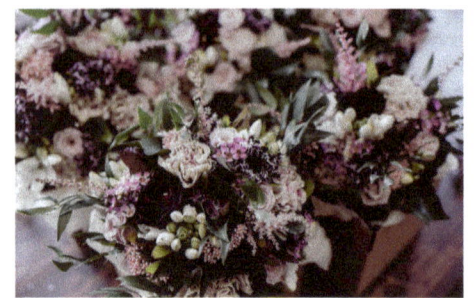

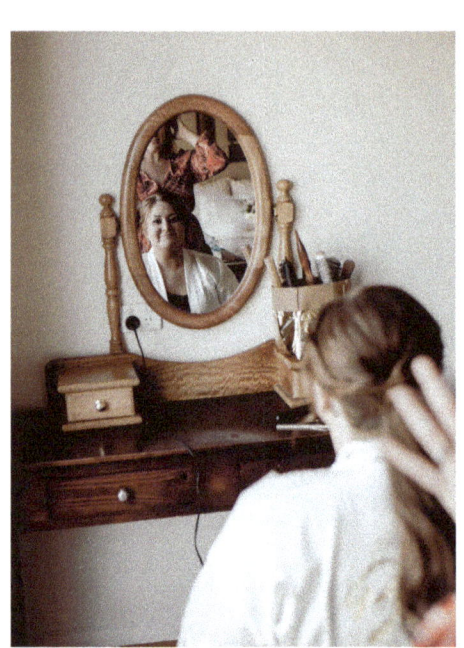

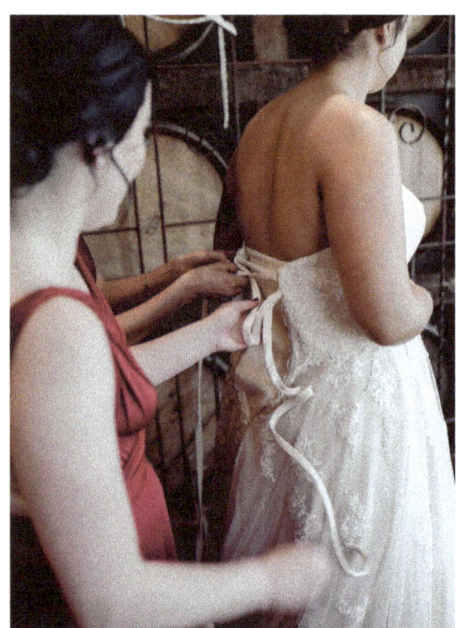

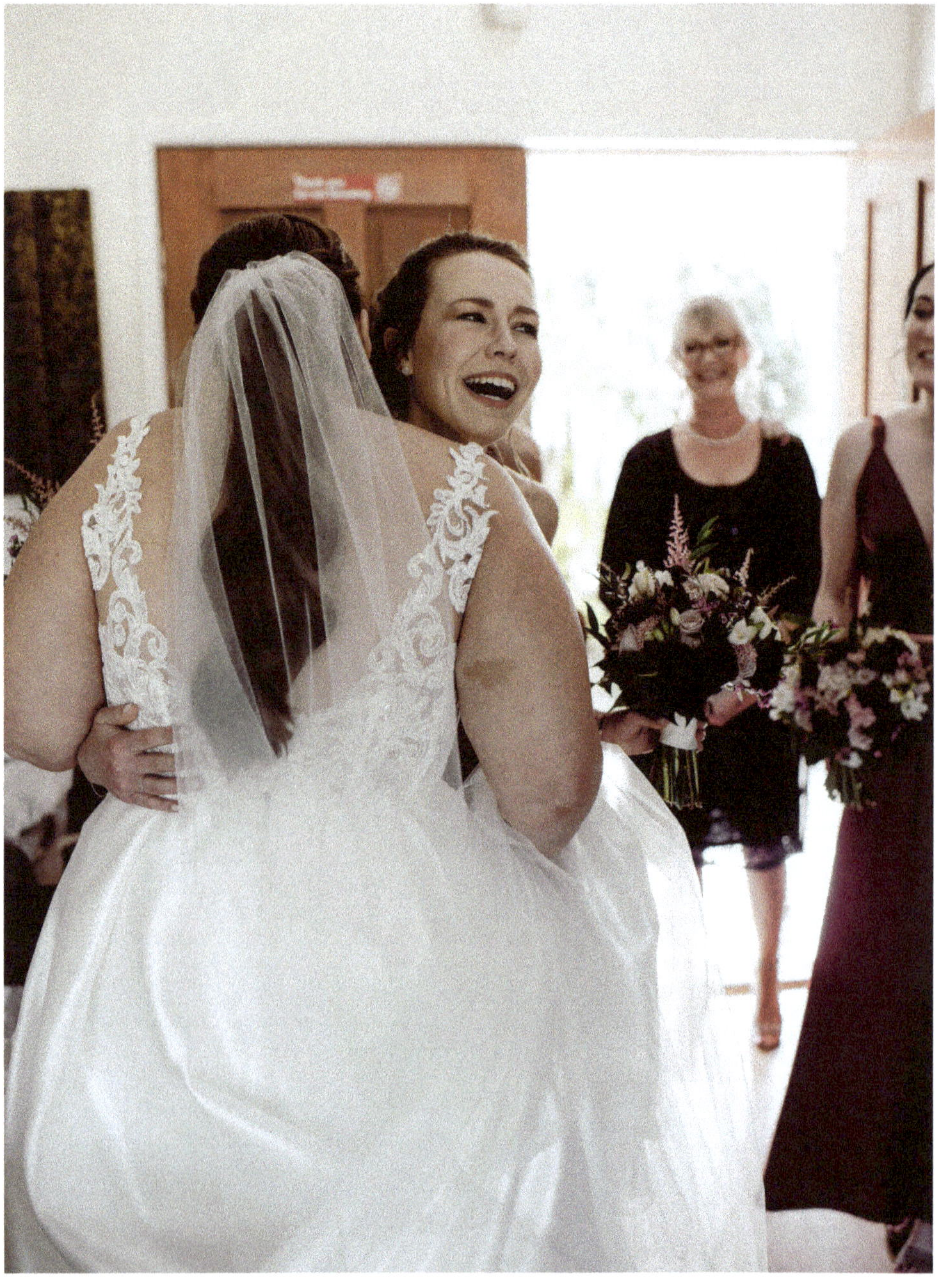

Abbey & Kate met on good old Tinder over three years ago, and enjoy a full and fun life. Between work, you could find them on hikes searching for hidden waterfalls or snuggled on the couch, eating nachos.

Their proposal unfolded on the night of Kate's graduation ball, during a late-night stroll through the botanical gardens. After kicking off their heels, they walked down some steps and found themselves in a little area enclosed by trees, flowers and a water feature. As a courageous Kate (who finds it hard to express her feelings) was describing everything she loves about Abbey and how her life had changed since meeting her... she took out the ring and proposed.

Abbey bawled her eyes out in a very ungracious way and said a big yes! When she calmed down, she then described all the reasons she wanted to marry Kate, and proposed straight back.

When the couple first got engaged, same-sex marriage was not legal in Australia. So, they planned to have a 'wedding' celebration here in Australia and then travel overseas to a country where same-sex marriage was legal and elope. However, after many unreturned emails from venues and vendors regarding their wedding request, the women admit that they felt hurt and disheartened.

Thanks to marriage equality laws changing in Australia, Abbey and Kate were able to start planning their wedding on home soil.

When it came to their wedding day, the couple didn't want anything to be uptight or rigid. They wanted it to reflect themselves and be fun, free and flowy. After choosing a rustic aesthetic with a laid-back vibe, they turned to Pinterest for inspiration and started planning.

Their venue was one that they hadn't previously looked at, however, it popped up on Kate's Facebook feed as an advertisement. The owners of the venue were so happy with the change of law that they had put on a special for same-sex couples who were wanting to now get legally married. So, they visited Immerse and fell in love with their vineyard chapel and their wonderful, welcoming staff.

After a few outfit hiccups, the brides-to-be both found their dream dresses at the same store, using the same consultant that guided them both to 'the moment' when you know you have found 'the one'.

Abbey and Kate spent the night before their wedding apart, and in the morning arrived at separate times at their venue to get ready with their family and bridal parties. Then, on a perfect Spring afternoon, the two brides thanked the weather gods and set forth to enjoy their wedding day, which they described as absolutely amazing.

Reflecting on their big day, both women reveal that they are glad they kept it very organic, with no over-dramatic statements or declarations of love, just what came naturally. Their exchange of vows was a perfect example of this, with both brides stating that their vows were so similar, they literally could have written one another's promises!

To Abbey and Kate, marriage represents unconditional love. Their wedding day showed them, and everyone else, just how well they know each other, as well as solidifying that they are 110% meant for each other.

"Some advice to those who are in the process of or thinking about planning their wedding as a same-sex couple: Your wedding is completely your own.

Don't let the media tell you what it 'should' be like. Don't let the search for the perfect venue or cake dishearten you because they don't agree with your sexuality, you will eventually find the perfect fit, it may take a bit longer but when you find it, it's 100% worth the wait."

Photography
James Thorne

Dresses
Stella York

Cake
Jessica's Cakes Brunswick

Florist
Jayne Egeberg

Hair
Emma Jean Bridal Hair

Makeup
Sian Howard Makeup, Crystal Meyer Makeup

Venue
Immerse Yarra Valley

RED HILL SOUTH, AUSTRALIA

JOEL & JOSEPH

PHOTOGRAPHY BY BE HERE BE NOW PHOTOS AND FILMS
www.beherebenow.com.au

"We have been together for so long that there was absolutely zero stress when it came to wedding planning.

We had massages, lunch and then our photographers came over and we took our dogs for a walk. The weather wasn't great and our ceremony was supposed to be outside so we were a little less than pleased with that, but what can you do?

Luckily, just as we arrived at the venue, the skies cleared and it was picture perfect.

From then on, it was exactly what we had imagined.

Even though, we have been together for quite some time, getting married felt like it has taken our commitment to a whole new level. I still get this butterfly feeling when I get to call him my husband."

Joel and Joseph have been together for an incredible 14 years. They met a short eight days after Joseph arrived in Australia, at 2am at the Market Nightclub in Prahran, which they sarcastically say was "very romantic". Nonetheless, it worked out perfectly for them!

The couple now live on Victoria's picturesque Mornington Peninsula with their two huskies and a cat. However, as Joel and Joseph love to travel, in was only fitting that their proposal took place on the other side of the world.

On a trip to Europe in 2018, they got engaged in Santorini while they were sitting on their balcony overlooking the Caldera at sunset in a moment that was 100% romantic.

It was a dream proposal that led into a year-long planning process for their big day. A process that they both recall as being extremely enjoyable and completely free from stress.

Both Joel and Joseph wanted their wedding to be at a winery on the peninsula. After lunching several times at the Red Hill Estate winery, they made their choice. For them it was the winery's incredible wine that tipped them over the edge.

In fact, having the wedding at a winery was the only thing they were set on for the wedding. Continuously calling themselves 'bad gays' throughout the process because they were so laid back about it. They put zero thought into the little details and focused on having a big party with all their family and friends... which is exactly what it turned out to be.

Outfit shopping turned out to be a fun event. The couple have a friend-of-a-friend who had just opened her own personal stylist business, so, they tasked her with dressing them. They met her at her family's house in Sorrento where she had a cheese platter and champagne waiting for them. She styled them in various suits until they found the right ones. Then, she customized them to perfection.

Their big day arrived and they spent the morning getting massages and lunch. Then their photographers from 'Be Here Be Now Photos and Films' came over and they took their dogs for a walk, which turned into an amazing first photo session.

The weather wasn't great and with their ceremony scheduled for outdoors, the grooms were a little less than pleased.

Luckily, just as they arrived at the venue, the skies cleared and it could not have been any more perfect. From then on, it was exactly what they had imagined.

The newlyweds first dance was one of their favorite moments of their day, which they made in honour of one of their best friends, who had sadly passed away. One of his favourite songs was Proud Mary by Tina Turner. Their first dance was to a sweet love song, but they cut it off 30 seconds in and put on Proud Mary and invited everyone up on the dance floor. It went off and was so amazing!

Fourteen years together did not take away any of the fresh new feels that getting married brings, and has taken Joel and Joseph's commitment to a whole new level.

Joel loves that he now gets that butterfly feeling whenever he calls Joseph 'my husband'.

Photographer
Be Here Be Now Photos and Film

Cake & Cake Topper
Peninsula Cake Art

Catering
Max's at Red Hill Estate

Celebrant
Emma Tomlinson

Cinematographer
Be Here Be Now Photos and Films

Entertainment
Dr Romeo

Event Stylist
Rose Vinci Styling

Florist
Poppies of Red Hill

Rings
Uniform Black

Venue
Max's at Red Hill Estate

PHOTOGRAPHY WITH DEPTH
magnoliaandember.com // worldwide travel
@magnoliaandember

How to choose your wedding vendors.

You're engaged! Congratulations!

Now, it's time to head down the rabbit hole of finding the perfect wedding suppliers to help bring to life what you envision your wedding day will be.

Which sounds fun, right? Until you realize that there are literally thousands of wedding pros out there to choose from - and it can get confusing.

From photographers to florists, event planners to the stationery designers, it can get overwhelming quickly - so, here's a little step by step guide to ease your way through the process.

1. Take your time
You're engaged, enjoy that bubble of excitement! There's no reason to jump onto locking in your vendors before you have done your homework. Celebrate being newly engaged with your lover - you deserve that. Go on dates, throw that engagement party and know that wedding planning will come in time.

2. Do your research
First things first, think about where you want to get married, the style and vibe you want the event to have and map out your budget.

The best way to go about this is to each sit-down and think about the three things you want to prioritize for your day - it might be photography, your wedding outfits, and your venue. Keep these at the top of mind when you are looking for vendors.

Find vendors through magazines, blogs, social media or word of mouth. Head to expos, if that is your scene.

3. Send you inquiries
Get your information ready and reach out to the wedding vendors who have made your 'we need to know more' list. You'll need; your names, contact details, wedding date, wedding location, and any questions that you want to ask.

Your initial inquiry is a good opportunity to see if you vibe with the wedding pro, make sure that they work within your budget, and that they are available on the date, you're hoping to marry.

4. Shortlist your vendors
If you've reached out to three different florists, it's now time to cull that list down to two (or one, if you can!).

If you have only reached out to one stylist who you're head over heels in love with, and you don't want to consider anyone else, it's totally okay to skip ahead and make a decision. Don't feel like you need to complicate things.

5. Arrange consultations
If you are having trouble really narrowing down your list, it might be time to book in for a face-to-face (or online/phone) consultations.

While it might not be necessary to arrange a consultation with all of your wedding vendors, we would recommend really catching up with your photographer and officiant at the very minimum. These are two wedding vendors that are going to play one of the most significant roles on your wedding day. You want these people to really understand your love story, and champion it.

6. Make your decisions
The most exciting part - it's time to lock in your chosen wedding vendors. Make sure you get in touch as soon as you've made a decision so that your wedding date is still available. It is commonplace that you'll need to pay a deposit before you can confirm your booking.

Before you do pay that deposit, it's your last chance to read over contracts and ask any questions.

You don't want to go into anything without knowing exactly where you stand.

And, it should go without saying, reach out to the wedding vendors who you have decided, for whatever reason, just aren't right for you. It's common courtesy. Don't stress about the wedding vendors taking offense; they will appreciate the honesty, we promise.

AN LOVE STORY

DEAN & SAM

PHOTOGRAPHY BY FOX & KIN
www.foxandkin.com

We wish we could say we met in a cute way like they do in the movies, but the truth is we met in a much cuter way; Tinder!

We decided to meet in person at a beach in Newcastle. The funny thing is, is that one of us thought it was halfway between our houses, while the other one of us knew this definitely was not the case!

Nonetheless, he made the drive from the Central Coast anyway (like a true gentleman). We both awkwardly, but excitedly, got to know each other while exploring Newcastle, and ended up with a pretty intense sunburn as a souvenir for the best first date ever.

Some of our favorite memories were in that time, when we first started seeing each other. We lived about an hour and a half away from each other, so the whole day would be spent waiting to begin the drive to the other person's house.

The best part was always walking through the front door and seeing the other person just as excited to see you. It was our own little escape from the world, just the two of us.

Like any relationship though, it hasn't always been roses.

The biggest challenge we've faced has been maintaining a good, healthy relationship, while one of us completed a university degree.

University degrees come along with their own fair share of challenges.

Combine stress, mental health, spending months away from each other over placement periods and pre and post-exam breakdowns. With a general lack of financial security, it is tough on one person, let alone adding a relationship into the mix.

Lucky for us, Dean is the most supportive, beautiful human in the entire world and took it all in his stride.

For Dean, his favorite thing about Sam is his unfettered love for plants, art, music, fashion, good food, and even board games. Before he met Sam, he never looked twice at plants or bothered to play a game of chess, etc. But since being together, Sam has taught Dean to look at these things in a new light, with a better understanding and appreciation for them. Now, Dean can't walk into a nursery without buying a plant!

For Sam, his favorite things about Dean are his infectious laughter, his positive outlook on life, his sense of adventure, and the way he listens to Dean's many rambling stories.

Dean has a tendency to get side-tracked easily, and a 5-minute fun fact turns into an entire breakdown of why each Harry Potter book is superior to each Harry Potter movie. But, most of all, he loves the warmth and love he gives him.

We both see ourselves traveling, buying a house, adopting more pets, getting married, and eventually having kids.

A note from the photographer: Fox & Kin

In celebration of pride month, I gave away an at-home shoot, and Dean and Sam were the couple who won. They rented out a super cute Airbnb, and we spent the afternoon hanging out and documenting their beautiful, playful and intense love.

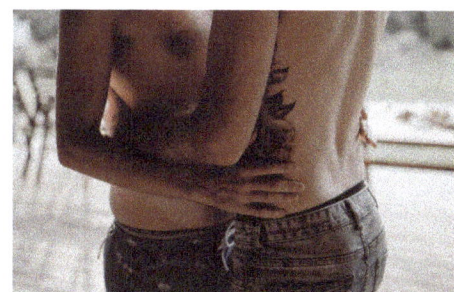

Photography by Gabriell Vieira

APOEMA
EVENTS

www.apoemaevents.com
Lisbon | Portugal
@apoemaevents

A PROPOSAL

LAUREN & ROYA

PHOTOGRAPHY BY KRISTYN TAULANE
www.kristyntaulane.com

Together, Lauren and Roya had purposely discussed the ins and outs of an engagement, before the proposal happened!

They are firm believers that both partners need to be on the same page when it comes to monumental life moments and milestones. While a proposal (that is a true surprise) sounded romantic to them, they both wanted to be confident that they were ready.

Ultimately, they had always known that they wanted to marry one another, so it was more a matter of when, than if. Then, after moving into a new place and receiving promotions at work, the timing just felt right.

They discussed who would propose to who, and Roya expressed interest in being the one to do both the planning and the asking. While Lauren knew it would be happening, she had no idea of how, or when it was happening.

It turned out, Roya already had the proposal in the works, for over a year.

As a surprise, Roya had orchestrated a couples photography shoot - one that would disguise the anticipated proposal.

The photographer, Kristyn, suggested the location, which was a nearby canyon. The original idea was to make the proposal at the beach, where they had their first date. However, Kristyn advised that beach pictures may be difficult, depending on the weather, and Roya wasn't prepared to take the risk.

A choice that paid off - their dream proposal was captured right at sunset.

Directly after the proposal, Roya took Lauren to a nearby restaurant for, what Lauren thought would be a small celebratory moment for us.

Lauren stood out the front, trying to call her parents to share the good news. She was unable to get through after multiple attempts and desperate texts to call her back, so, Roya convinced Lauren to try from inside the restaurant.

On walking in, Lauren quickly realized the entire room was filled with their loved ones - Lauren's parents included. It turns out while Lauren was making those frantic phone calls from just outside the restaurant, Roya was texting them not to answer their phones. Both of their families were there, as well as their friends from all over the country.

Roya had secretly been in contact with them, coordinating flights, and organizing the surprise.

Neither Lauren or Roya wanted a traditional diamond ring for ethical reasons, but they loved the look of moissanite, so that choice was perfect. Both rings have a beautiful rose gold setting.

Lauren found the rings and shared them with Roya prior to the proposal, to give her an idea of what she would like. However, even more special than the ring, was the box that Roya chose to place it in.

The lid of the box was adorned with wooden carvings of our two cats, and the interior of the box said "Meowy Me." A special little reminder of the life they have already built together.

For the lovers, their engagement represents their shared goal of spending their lives together.

A LOVE STORY

BOBBY & JOEL

PHOTOGRAPHY BY SILK AND THORN
www.silkandthorn.com

How did you meet?
B & J: We meet in an English class twelve years ago while pursuing our undergraduate degrees. We became great friends on social media and made our relationship official a number of months later. We have been inseparable ever since. We would spend hours talking on the phone late at night just getting to know each other, we're best friends first which is the beautiful foundation our relationship has been built upon.

What is your favorite memory together?
B: I have so many, however my favorite memory would be a week-long trip we took to New York in December of 2012. My family lives in New York so I never have experienced New York through the eyes of someone who has never been. That was Joel's first real trip to the states capital, we went to our first Broadway show, saw Jay-Z for the first time and tried every cuisine New York had to offer.

J: I would have to say my favorite memory would be our birthday celebrations. We both believe birthdays should be celebrated in a grand way. So each year we design a cake for the others birthday that fits the theme of that year's party. We keep the cake design secret so its a surprise you get to enjoy for your birthday. This is something I greatly enjoy and always look forward to every year!

As you can imagine we've spent many birthdays together so we've had some beautiful cakes made each year.

What's been some of the harder things you've had to overcome together?
B: I believe the biggest challenge we had to overcome was when we lived apart for three years, we were tested in every way possible.

I was in grad school and Joel, had taken a new job. Those three years forced us to really do some self-exploration and face some major fears head-on. I believe it was during that time that we truly understood the meaning of unconditional love, and in turn our love for one another.

J: I completely agree with Bobby, those three years away were some of the most trying times of our relationship. Meeting each other while we were so young we hardly knew ourselves, the time apart was filled with us discovering ourselves as adults outside of college life. We learned so much about ourselves, and it gave us an opportunity to come back together and grow from the young boys that met, to the young men we are today.

What is your favorite thing about one another?
B: My favorite thing about Joel is the fact that he is my best friend, he gets me like no one else does and I know he has my back. I also admire and respect his creative ability, I've never met someone who is good at almost everything they do.

J: My favorite thing about Bobby is his love for music, he lights up when it comes to anything music. From the fashion, the stage design at the concerts, the musical arrangements, and production. Bobby would always make mixed CDs or playlists of music for me, I would always be excited to hear the new music he'd mix together just for me.

And, what does the future hold for you both?
B & J: First is our marriage in August 2020. Then, possibly children. Most importantly though, it'll be growing together, traveling the world and starting a business.

INSPIRATION

BRIGHTON ROMANCE

PHOTOGRAPHY BY STEPHANIE DREAMS PHOTOGRAPHY
www.stephaniedreamsphotography.com

A note from the photographer:

"This shoot was all about fun, love and honestly, what I hope for every wedding of mine to be. I wanted it to capture what LGBTQ+ means to me.

Being a 'late-life lesbian' has really opened my eyes to making LGBTQ+ couples more visible and the need to normalize, things like getting married.

The rainbow veil was actually what the whole shoot was based around. When I saw that beauty from Crown & Glory, I knew it would be a big part of the photoshoot and overall look of what I wanted to achieve.

From there, the majority of my ideas came from pastel rainbow colors, whilst adding in fun floristry as well as vintage ideas and styling. The cake and sweet grazing table was a big idea for us, all the colors and textures worked so well together, and the vintage styling table connected everything so well.

The veil worked perfectly with the dress, with its simple, but beautiful features the veil had a moment of its own.

It is all a perfect blend of styles, it feels sweet and pretty, whilst being cool too. The vintage vibes of the ceremony and top table, especially, made the relaxed but fun look all come together.

Although the weather was against us, getting out in Brighton was still so much fun & also so important to show couples to make the most of their day- no matter the weather. Being in between a few different storms, photographing on the pier still worked well, with the girls putting on their converse and jackets for a more relaxed look.

Megan & Whitney's love shines through on every single photo; they were such a joy to photograph and made the shoot come together seamlessly"

Photography & Concept
Stephanie Dreams Photography

Cake
Charlotte Anne Cake Design

Celebrant
Perfect Words Ceremonies

Dresses
Matchimony

Lovers
Megan & Whitney (What Wegan Did Next)

Makeup
Nadia Wyatt H&MU

Musician
Robynne Calvert Music

Painted Jackets
Creations by Miss Molly

Perspex Signs
Petitjeans Designs

Planning & Floristry
Hire Societies

Stationery
Made by Rae Designs

Styling & Props
Betty Loves Vintage

Veil
Crown and Glory

Videography
JDP Photography

AUSTRALIA

FLOWERS IN NATURE
Florals

If you're looking for something a little more unique, rustic and sustainable, Flowers In Nature would love to discuss our dried flowers with you!

www.flowersinnature.com.au
@flowersinnature.everlastings

STYLE LE AISLE
Planner & Stylist

Attentive, creative and extremely personable, Style Le Aisle possess a clear and creative outlook, as well as a true passion, for individually styling their clients' most cherished celebrations.

www.styleleaisle.com.au
@styleleaisle

FOX & HART
Stationery & Signage

We are a wedding design studio where the whimsical meets the rebel-hearted. We specialise in calligraphy, signage and stationery for those who colour outside the lines.

www.foxandhart.com.au
@foxandhart

GATHERING EVENTS
Catering

Bring your special day to life with our interactive bars, food carts, coffee carts and gelato carts. Serving Brisbane and Adelaide, our diverse catering offers signature cocktails to a tantalising food menu, bringing good old fashioned service to your special day.

www.gatheringevents.com.au
@gathering_events

PRESSED PANTRY
Catering

Pressed Pantry is Barossa Valley's boutique catering, food artistry and styling business, created by two sisters through the love of food and wine.

www.pressedpantry.com.au
@pressedpantry

TUESDAY PHOTOGRAPHY
Photography

Tuesday Photography is based in Brisbane and available nationwide. Jess has a passion for creating beautiful images and capturing the magic of her couples.

www.tuesdayphotography.com.au
@ohheytuesday

JESSICA JOSIE PHOTOGRAPHY
Photography

Photography that values authenticity above all else; for couples who aren't afraid of a double chin laugh or an ugly cry; for images filled with your joy and one-of-a-kind love.

www.jessicajosiephotographer.com.au
@jessicajosiephotographer

E SQUARED DESIGN CO.
Florist & Styling

E Squared Design Co. is best known for their innovative, sumptuous and intuitive florals and styling. Producing immersive and inspiring affairs, they are a versatile team who are inventive and passionate when it comes to styling your wedding or event.

www.esquareddesignco.com
@esquareddesignco

UNITED STATES OF AMERICA

WILDLY COLLECTIVE
Planning & Design

Wildly Collective is a design and planning company for weddings and elopements. They focus on connection: to your values, to your love, to the outdoors, to breaking and creating traditions, to your wildly unique story.

www.wildlycollective.com
@wildlycollective_

VILLANELLE FLORAL
Florist

The heart of Villanelle is creating floral interpretations of personal stories. They develop custom floral arrangements that leave clients feeling sought-after, understood, and accepted -- and hopefully a little more in touch with the primal beauty of the natural world.

www.villanellefloral.com
@villanellefloral

AMARIE FLORA
Florist

Floral design studio based in Portland, Oregon crafting immersive living installations which transform environments and elevate human experience for intimate gatherings, weddings, editorials and workshops. They are botanical artists—bringing inspired floral interpretations to life in celebration of love and beauty.

www.amarieflora.com
@amarie_flora

ANNAMAE PHOTO
Photography

For Annamae Photo there is something so beautiful about combining nature and human connection. I am moved by love and the fact that this is what I do for work makes me grateful beyond words. Keep loving!

www.annamaephoto.com
@itsannamaephoto

AIDE MEMOIRE JEWELRY
Jewelry

Aide-mémoire Jewelry is an all-inclusive, queer woman-owned small business in Seattle, Washington. We focus on handmade, eco-friendly, and conflict-free everyday fine jewelry, wedding bands, and engagement rings.

www.aidememoirejewelry.com
@aidememoirejewelry

THE BOLD AMERICAN
Photography

Marriage is celebrating love for one another and the willingness to accept each other's strengths and weaknesses. It's about sharing our individual outlooks and growing through our shared experiences.

www.the-bold-americana.com
@theboldamericana

DANIELLE NICOLE
Photography

Danielle Nicole is a couples photographer based in Oregon & California. They travel all over the country creating space for their clients to share their most intimate and connected moments regardless of orientation - amazed that they get to capture the magic in everyone's lives.

www.daniellenicole.photography
@daniellenicolespage

BAGEL'S FLORALS
Florist

Bagel's Florals makes exquisite floral creations that are as unique as you and your special day. Queer-owned and operated, Bagel's Florals is the perfect choice for those looking for an artist-florist with a fresh and inspired approach to design.

www.bagelsflorals.com
@bagelsflorals

AROUND THE WORLD

ALVARO SANCHA
Photography

I love my job as a wedding photographer, making wedding shoots and couple sessions, where I have the opportunity to meet wonderful couples, where I create a great connection with them and I can create one of the best memories for a lifetime.

www.alvarosancha.com
@alvarosancha

MY ONE AND ONLY
Photography

My One and Only is born from our historia of love. We love to build emotive and natural memories that are remembered for the rest of life. We believe in free love without any kind of barriers. Love is love nothing more and nothing less.

www.myoneandonlywpaf.com
@myoneandonlywpaf

TÜELL & TASSEL
Stationery

A Berlin-based studio, creating stationery for your dream wedding. Because we love continuity throughout the whole wedding design, we also decorate weddings in and around Berlin: stationery, table setting, flowers, a balloon decorations from a single source, will create the perfect, harmonious setting for your big day.

www.tuell-tassel.de
@tuelltassel

CAKES BERLIN
Cakes

Known for brave color combinations and funky style, cakes Berlin is the chosen cake studio for Berliner couples who don't shy away from a bit of pizzazz in their wedding.

www.cakesberlin.com
@cakesberlin

THE MARRY MAKER
Ceremonies

A symbolic wedding ceremony held by The Marry Maker is the perfect way to celebrate your love – regardless of your nationality, religious beliefs or sexual orientation. There are no predefined standards or specifications. Everything will be arranged completely according to your preferences.

www.themarrymaker.com
@the.marry.maker

APOEMA EVENTS
Planner & Stylist

The word APOEMA, is derived from an indigenous word, meaning the ability to see beyond what lies ahead, this is what we are based on and aligned with. Based in Lisbon, we bring life, color, and creativity to every personlized wedding consultation.

www.apoemaevents.com
@apoemaevents

PATRICIA HENDRYCHOVA ESTANGUET
Photography

Discover the intimate world of Patricia Hendrychova-Estanguet's photographs inspired by light and nature. Her sensitive and delicate eye sublimate each of her subjects. She is a photographer of intimate weddings, fashion & portrait in southwest of France and everywhere the adventure brings her.

www.patriciahendrychovaestanguet.com
@patriciahendrychovaestanguet

JOY ZAMORA
Photography

I'm a destination wedding photographer based in the south of Spain, my aim is to capture the reality of love in every single aspect and to create a meaningful connection with the stories behind my couples. My passion is to photograph intimate and emotional weddings around the world.

www.joyzamora.com
@darkmaito

Photo By Tessa Follett

Photo By Shari + Mike

RUPERT

www.rupertonrupert.com.au
@rupertonrupert

www.ingramcontent.com/pod-product-compliance
Lightning Source LLC
Chambersburg PA
CBHW042040040526
44107CB00095B/2997